SCHIRMER'S LIBRARY
OF MUSICAL CLASSICS

T0066477

Vol. 2127

THREE ROMANTIC PIANO CONCERTOS

Schumann: Piano Concerto in A minor, Op. 54

Grieg: Piano Concerto in A minor, Op. 16

Rachmaninoff: Piano Concerto No. 2 in C minor, Op. 18

ISBN 978-1-4950-8077-7

G. SCHIRMER, Inc.

DISTRIBUTED BY

HAL•LEONARD®

7777 W. BLUEMOUND RD. P.O. BOX 13819 MILWAUKEE, WI 53213

www.musicsalesclassical.com
www.halleonard.com

CONTENTS

Dedicated to Ferdinand Hiller

Piano Concerto in A minor
Op. 54

Edited by
Edwin Hughes

Robert Schumann

6

15

16

18

32

34

Vcello and Bass pizz.

Cadenza (♩ = former ♪)

Un poco andante

45

Intermezzo
Andante grazioso (♪ = 120)

Viola and V'cello

Bass and Bassoon

58

Allegro vivace (♩. = 80)

una corda

69

73

91

Dedicated to Edmund Neupert

Piano Concerto in A minor

Op. 16

Edited, revised, fingered, pedaled,
and with explanatory remarks,
by Percy Grainger

Edvard Grieg

*)The 32ds should be played *pp*, like delicate grace-notes.

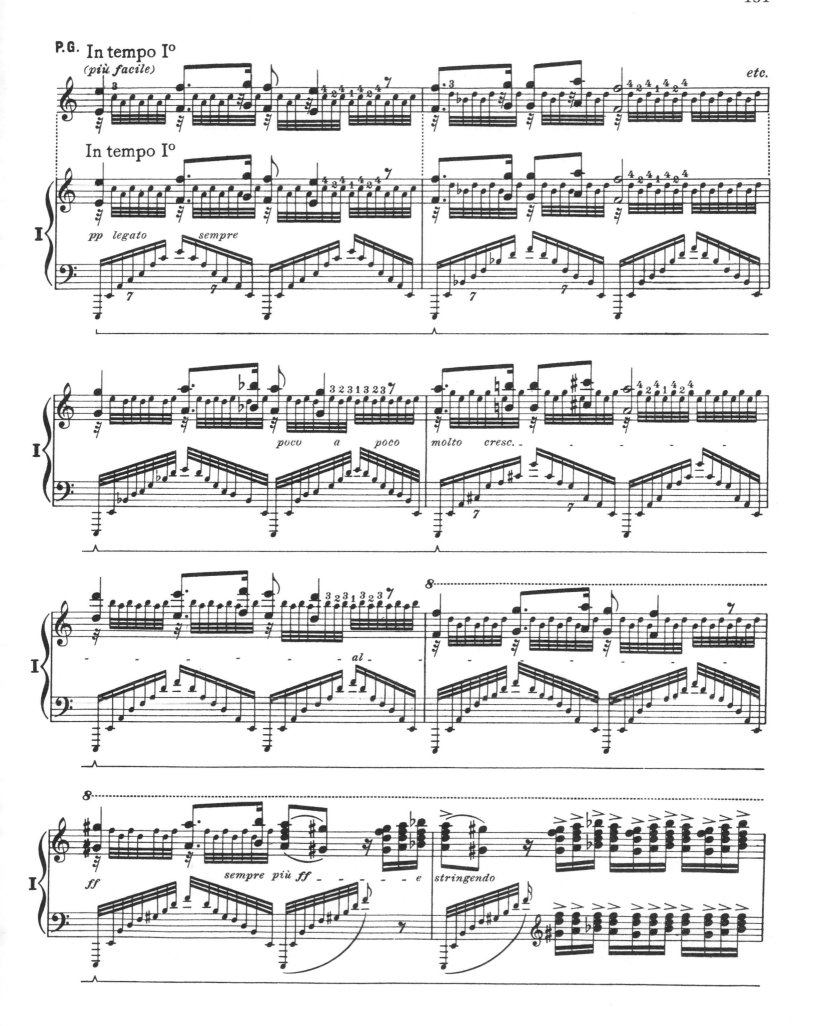

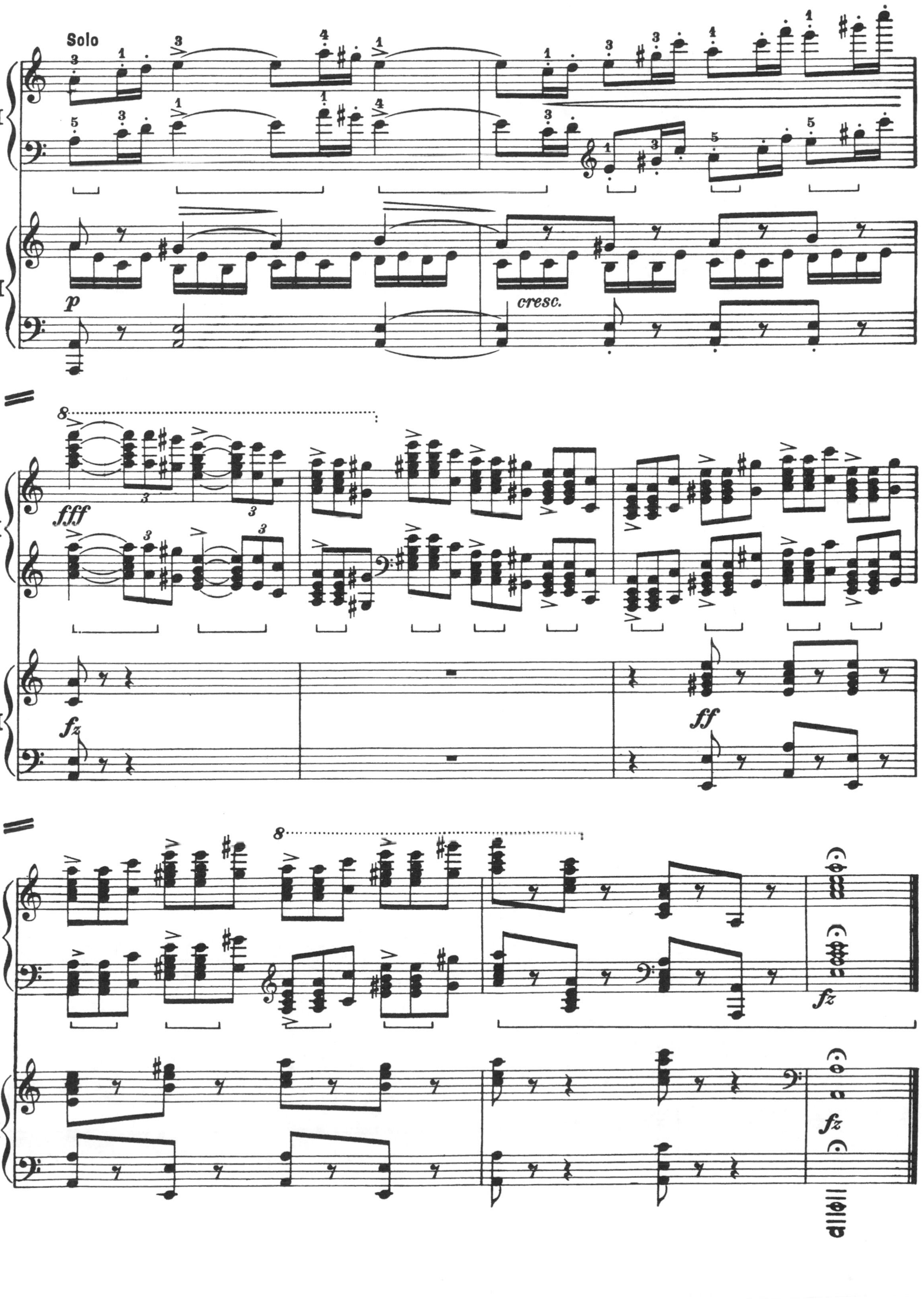
Solo
I
II
p
cresc.
fff
fz
ff
fz
fz

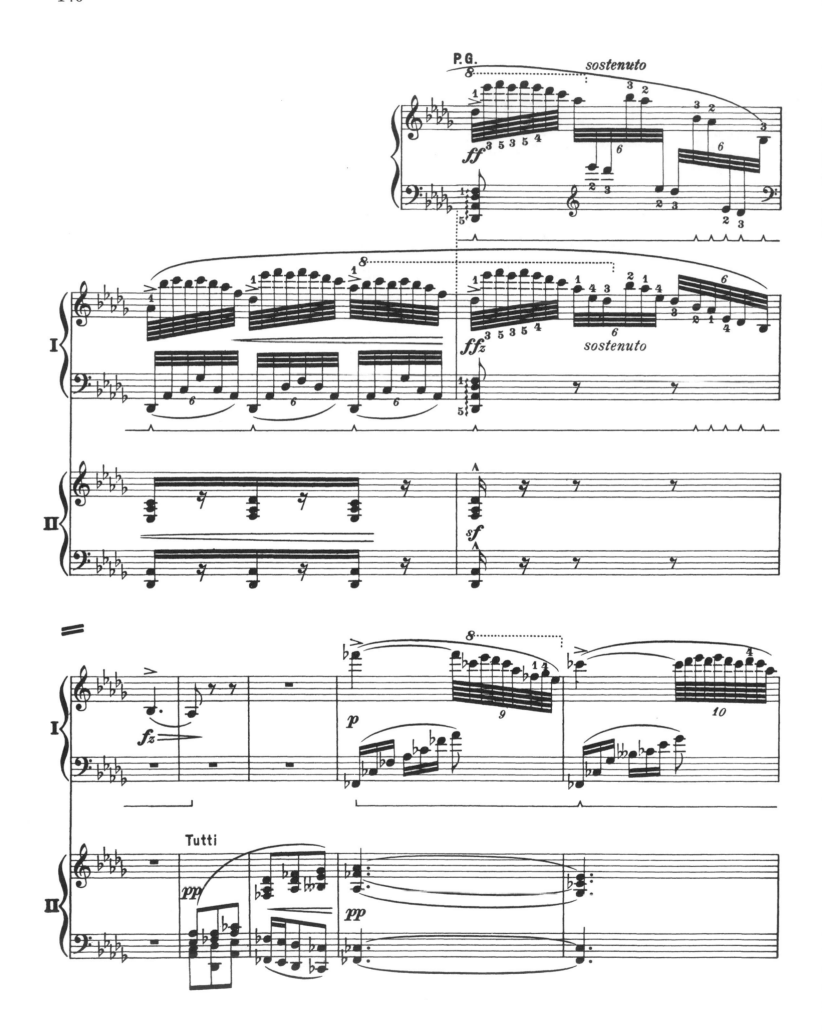

144

145

Grieg played the melody note E♭(at ✱) so loudly and the bass octave B♭♭(at ✱✱) so softly that at ✱✱ the former could clearly be heard singing on above the latter.

146

When playing with orchestra the pianist can execute the measure before the "poco animato" (which has a pause in Piano II) by regulating its duration as if it were two measures instead of one, duly advising the conductor in advance. By this means it is easier for the conductor to bring in the chord of the full orchestra exactly together with the last note of the pianist's run. The same applies to the runs in Piano I and the pauses in Piano II occuring one measure before A and one measure before F. The conductor should be advised in advance in all three cases.

Grieg wished the melodic basis of this passage, F#, F♮, E, to be very prominently heard.

The following rhythmic division of the passage-work was recommended to the editor by his teacher Professor James Kwast, as being advisable, in the interests of clarity and accuracy, owing to the rapid tempo of the movement.

154

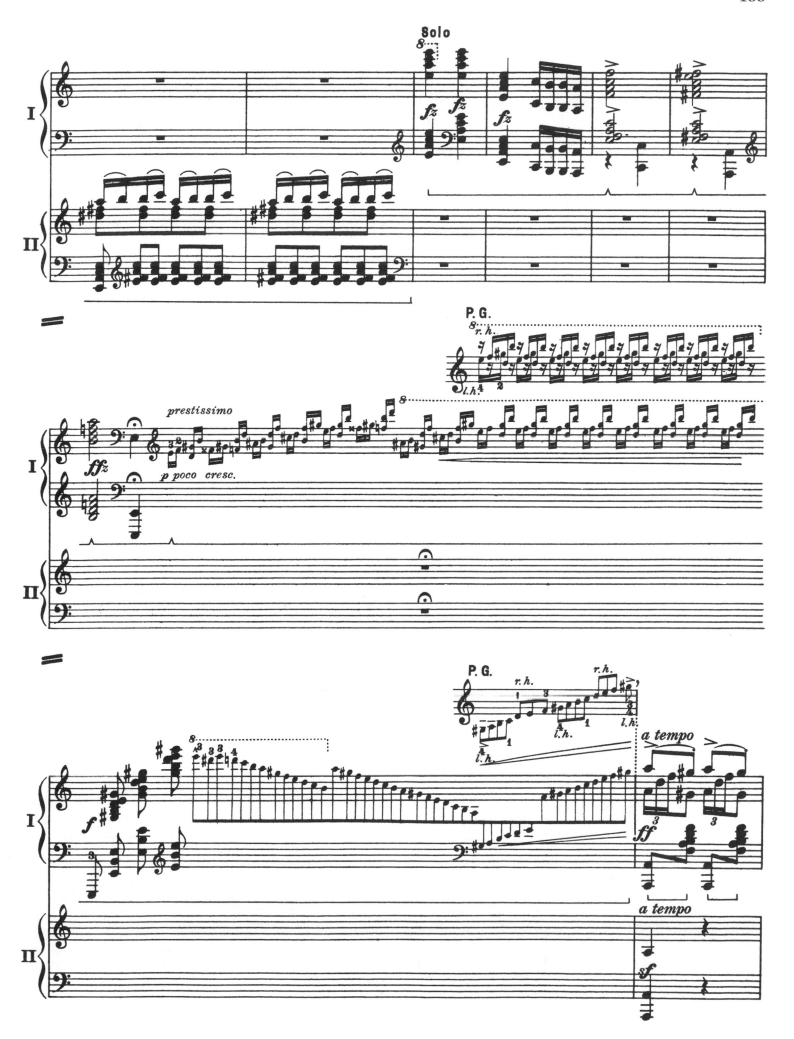

159

Poco piu tranquillo (♩ = 92)

Poco più tranquillo (♩ = 92)

160

Editor's note. Grieg played the following solo with restless, almost feverish emotionality, but without a trace of sentimentality. The louds and softs were very dramatically contrasted in his rendering of this section, and *tempo rubato* was freely used, without, however, the general speed being reduced from about M. M. ♩ = 92.

Recommended to the editor
by Professor James Kwast

179

182

184

à Monsieur N. Dahl

Piano Concerto No. 2 in C minor
Op. 18

Sergei Rachmaninoff

I.

II.

211

214

III.

Allegro scherzando. (Moto primo.) ($\textnormal{♩} = 116.$)